TAP IN

BRICK-BY-BRICK

TAPPING INTO YOUR HIGHER POWER

By: Eligha Pryor *with Don West, Jr.*

Tap In
Brick-By-Brick
Tapping Into Your Higher Power

A Memoir Chronicling Lessons
From the Life & journeys of Eligha L. Pryor, Jr.

© 2023 by Eligha L. Pryor, Jr.

All rights reserved. No part of this book may be reproduced in any form or by any electronic or mechanical means including information storage and retrieval systems – except in the case of brief quotations embodied in critical articles or reviews – without permission in writing from its publisher, Axis Publishing & Distribution Company, LLC.

First Edition, 2023

Published by:
Axis Publishing & Distribution Company, LLC

Printed in the **United States of America**
ISBN: 978-0-9822479-4-5

Contents

Introduction iv

Who is Eligha Pryor, now? vi

Chapter 1 | A Fancy Night Out On The Town 1

Chapter 2 | The Downfall 10

Chapter 3 | News About Your Father 20

Chapter 4 | One Of The Fastest Masons In The World 27

Chapter 5 | Don't Forget Where You Come From 34

Chapter 6 | Support Systems, Mentors & the Importance of Mentorship 41

Chapter 7 | Mindset & Revelation 59

Chapter 8 | The Work 68

Chapter 9 | Don't Give Up – Never Quit 72

Introduction

"'E.P. All Day' because I am going to be my authentic self, all day."

~E.P.

I started doing speaking engagements a few years ago sharing my experiences and lessons from my life. At these engagements, people often ask me if I have a book they can buy or order online. My answer has always been, "not yet." Now that answer has changed.

I wrote this book in hopes of helping someone by sharing my story and some of the lessons I have learned along the way. I write about things that are important to me, my dad who has been my hero since I was a young boy, my work and business, my wife and family, and some of the people who have helped and mentored me along the way.

When speaking I often say, "there must be a sacrifice because it is not going to be easy." Writing this book was no exception. Like many goals that we set for ourselves, it took time and at times I had to overcome my mental hurdles. Deciding what to share and how to say and write about my life was no easy task.

But you are here reading this page and that is a tremendous blessing for me, and I appreciate you investing your time to read my words and thoughts. May you find something special in these pages, perhaps the inspiration you need to tap into your own God-given potential and power.

Let's go – let's grow!

You are a special gift from God, believe in yourself and build yourself up to success just like a wall to any house or building, brick-by-brick. Enjoy the book and no matter what, don't ever give up hope or faith.

Tapped in and on the grind,

E.P. – "All Day"

Who is Eligha Pryor, now?

He is a:

1. Father;
2. Husband;
3. Masonry Contractor;
4. General Contractor;
5. Mortgage Broker;
6. Real Estate Investor;
7. Insurance Agent;
8. Private Investor;
9. Motivational Speaker;

and,

10. *Award-Winning Author.*

Chapter 1

A Fancy Night Out On The Town

Keep Your Business to Yourself

&

Let Your Success Speak for Itself

Greetings reader, my name is Dina[1] and I am what many people call an Angel. Now it may seem odd that we are here together in Eligha's master bedroom closet, but as I continue to tell you the fantastic story of what is about to happen to Eligha after he leaves this closet tonight; you will have a much better grasp of why we started here in the closet right before Eligha and his fiancé head out for a special night on the town. I am guessing some of you are wondering who is this guy, Eligha, and why is there an Angel in his closet telling us a story?

Well… I have been observing and watching over Eligha since he was born, and the story of his journey is simply one of my favorites of all time. It is a classic tale of loss,

---

[1] Dina – the angel of learning. This celestial being is said to be the angel who taught humans how to speak. He continually inspires us to culturally evolve and fills our hearts with love of learning.

transformation, and redemption. I am betting you will agree as well once you have heard his entire inspirational story.

Let me share a little more background here, since Eligha was born he bore the birthright of an especially gifted and favored young man. You see, Eligha Lewis Pryor, Jr. was born May 15, 1975, in a small south Florida community to Eligha, Sr. and Shirley Pryor. Eligha grew up in a small town in the Southeastern part of the state of Florida. Eligha is his father's eldest son, the fourth of six children, and Eligha has always looked up to and admired his father from day one.

When Eligha was born his father was a prominent and successful masonry contractor. His father owned a successful business and had several people that worked for him on his crew. Eligha's father built his business from the ground up. His father had dropped out of school in the fifth grade and yet due to his skills as a mason, he was able to grow a successful multi-million-dollar construction business that built houses, office buildings, and even schools. From the time Eligha was three years old, in part because he was his dad's first son, his father would take him everywhere with him. Eligha was like his dad's shadow, especially at work.

Eligha was a bright and attentive young man and while at work with his dad he watched and learned from his father and his father's crew. Eligha did not know it at the time, but a special part of his favor was that he was built to be a mason. He was created with the natural born gifts that paved the way for him to become a master of laying extremely large and heavy concrete blocks. In short, Eligha is built like a "bull" or a "brick house" as they say.

Even as a young man he had the perfect large bone structure to support and carry heavy cinder blocks and bricks and even more impressive were the bulges of muscle that wrapped and stretched from every inch of his massive frame. We angels joke all the time, it was like someone ordered a Power Lifter on the day Eligha was born, and God decided to deliver a prototypical model of physical strength, size, and excellence the day Eligha came into this world. Hopefully, you now have a clear picture; Eligha has always been "Big" and "Strong," the perfect combination for an aspiring mason.

Eligha took his physical gifts even further, he would observe his father and his father's workers and take away their best traits as masons. By the time he was 8 years old he was able to finish concrete slabs by himself and thus he was an 8-year-old concrete finisher. When Eligha was in 8th grade he made a firm determination in his mind, he decided he wanted to be like his dad. He wanted to become a masonry contractor.

His dad was successful, his dad was able to provide for the family, and his dad always had lots of money coming across the table. After tenth grade, at 15 years old, Eligha found himself bored with school, and in love with an older woman he knew outside of school and because of these things he convinced his parents to allow him to quit school, get his own apartment, and he started working for his dad full-time. Eligha was so in love with the older woman that he threatened his parents that if they did not allow him to move out, he would kill himself. Not wanting such a tragic result his parents allowed him to make the move.

For the next couple of years, he worked for his father and fine-tuned his masonry skills. Two years later, at a mere 17 years old he was made the foreman of his father's crew. About a year later, at 18 years old, Eligha stopped working for his father and struck out on his own. He took and passed the county's exam and got a masonry contractor license, starting his own masonry business just like his father. Like many young black men of this era, he was motivated by the images broadcast on *Yo MTV Raps* and showcased by the "dope boys"[2] around the hood – he desired cool cars, nice clothes, and all the "benefits" of being successful. Unlike many others, Eligha had his father as a role model, and he had learned and was mastering his skills as a masonry contractor, which allowed him to legitimately bring in an income that put him on the same earning level and often ahead of the rappers on tv and the "dope boys" in the hood.

In his first year of business on his own, at only 19 years of age, Eligha was earning more than $4.5 million per year. Eligha's business thrived and he grew as a masonry contractor. He spent his time running and growing the business for several years always observing and learning new aspects of the construction game on the jobs he was working. He likes to say, "I mastered it," referring to being

---

[2] **Dope boys** – a term mostly used in southern parts of the US to describe any person who distributes illicit substances. Most often used to describe a young male that sells hard drugs (ex. cocaine, crack).

a masonry contractor. Because he felt he had mastered the masonry aspect of home building, he desired to step it up a little bit and build an entire home.

There was a local general contractor whom he worked with as a sub-contractor doing masonry work and Eligha started to desire to be more like him. He wanted to not only build the entire home from the ground up, but he wanted to be able to ride around in his Mercedes Benz or his Cadillac and tell another man, I have a job for you over here. And that is exactly what he did. Feeling he had mastered the masonry aspects of homebuilding, at 21 years old Eligha took the county's exam, passed, and became a licensed Residential Contractor. As a residential contractor, he was now able to take the lead and build the entire 2-story home from the ground up.

Eligha found fast success as a residential home builder. He crafted his business to deliver homes fast and at a market-advantaged price point. Because of his experience as a masonry contractor, he was able to hire and maintain the crews necessary not to have to engage sub-contractors and this enabled him to deliver a home in approximately 45 days from start to finish.

An eager and able-bodied learner, with the assistance of a bright young man in the area, Eligha embarked to teach himself how to use a CAD[3] software program to begin to make his own architectural adjustments and renderings.

---

[3] **Computer-aided design (CAD)** is the use of computers (or workstations) to aid in the creation, modification, analysis, or optimization of a design. It is the common method used by architects to design homes and other building structures.

Within a month, Eligha was competent on the CAD program, and he began to develop his own custom home designs.

At the age of 26 he built and opened his first model home center in his hometown. The fact that he was operating the first "black-owned" model home center in his hometown began to garner a lot of attention for Eligha, not all of it good or with good intentions. All types of people in the community began to wonder who is this guy and how is he able to do the things he is doing; especially, how does he have a model home center? While the community wondered and whispered, Eligha continued to work and prosper.

While his business life was in full swing, Eligha encountered a personal challenge in his first marriage that eventually resulted in a divorce. The divorce was contentious and at the center of the dispute was what would happen to the 7,800 square foot dream home sitting on five acres that Eligha had begun construction on prior to the divorce. When the marriage started having serious issues all construction on the property was stalled. Eligha's ex and her attorney both made great efforts during the divorce proceedings to take the property away from him.

In the end, the divorce was finalized and Eligha retained possession of the incomplete mansion. Following the divorce, understandably, Eligha was shaken and at the same time he was overcome with the desire to show his ex-wife and the world that the divorce had not broken him, nor his stride and he determined that the best way to do this was to complete construction on his dream home. And that is exactly what he did.

Eligha literally built this big ole 7,800 square foot house out of spite. He needed to show his ex-wife and anyone else looking that he was OK. Within forty-five days after the divorce was finalized construction on his dream home was in full swing. He worked hard to have the house finished, in fact it only took 10 ½ months to complete the construction after he started again. His dad told him, "People are not going to understand how you are building this big ole house." Eligha told his father, "I need to get out from under your shadow; I want to own something that is mine. I want to show the world who I am."

Looking back when asked what he should have done after his divorce Eligha says, "I should have gone into a shell and worked on rebuilding myself. I should not have worried about building a structure just to prove a point. I should have put my time and energy into finding my inner joy, I should have worked to find my inner peace." Ironically, Eligha found no joy or peace in the process of completing his dream home. He did not enjoy the process of completing the home, in fact he did not like any part of the work required to finish his home.

Sometimes in life we suffer inner hurts and pains, this is exactly what happened to Eligha when his first divorce happened. Eligha's hurts and pains mostly centered around the feelings associated with not being able to see his children. And like so many, instead of allowing the space for these hurts to exist and live with them, we seek to mask or hide them from ourselves and the outside world. We look for something to distract us and others from what is really happening on the inside. And that is exactly what Eligha did with his dream mansion. He convinced himself that finishing his dream home would show "Her" and everyone else that he was not phased. So, build and finish he did.

The mansion is one of a kind. It stands alone as one of the largest residential structures on the non-beach-side of his coastal hometown. And keep in mind all the folks in town are wondering how this young, black, mid-twenties gentleman named Eligha can build and afford such an opulent structure for himself. Many simply thought, "he is a drug dealer." And yet, he is not.

So, here we are, in the master bedroom closet of Eligha's 7,800 square foot dream home. And this closet is magnificent. Think of any movie scene with an amazing closet. This closet is probably nicer than any one you can conjure from memory and Eligha is finishing getting dressed for a special dinner on the "beach side" of town. And just in case you have not figured it out, the "beach side" is the fancy side of town, the privileged side. And because it is a special night, Eligha and his fiancé are headed to a exclusive spot for a fancy evening simply because they want to, and they can.

Both were dressed to kill. Eligha's fiance wearing an elegant and attractive number and Eligha decked out in slacks and a long sleeve button down shirt custom tailored to hug and accentuate his massive neck, shoulders, and arms. They looked impressive, the attention to detail in their outfits screamed sophistication and of course they simply looked like money.

While sitting at dinner Eligha spotted one of the city's more prominent older white residential developers at a nearby table and both acknowledged each other politely across the room. Eligha and his fiancé continued their meal and engaged in pleasant celebratory conversation when Eligha spots the gentleman approaching. Within moments he was at their table and engaging them in conversation. Suddenly and unexpectantly, the conversational tide turns, and the older white developer asked a pointed and direct question to Eligha. Hearing the question, his fiancé does all she can to prevent Eligha from engaging the older developer, she even nudges Eligha several times with her elbow, but her efforts are in vain. The older gentleman asks, "Have you made your first million dollars yet?" With an intense amount of pride and purpose Eligha straightens up and answers, "a long time ago."

With an intensity and direct maliciousness that shook Eligha and fiancé to their core the older white developer peered into Eligha's eyes and said, "You will never make another million dollars in this town." And he turned and walked away from their table.

Chapter 2

The Downfall

Downfalls happen- you can't stay down; you must get up.

"I had always been taught and I do believe that the Truth Shall Set You Free."

~ E.P.

Eligha and his fiancé finished their meal in virtual shocked silence as the words of the older gentleman soaked deep into the crevices of their minds. Eligha thought to himself momentarily that he should have kept his business to himself and simply allowed his work to speak for itself. But then again, he had nothing to hide and as they say, "the truth shall set you free."

As they drove home the incident faded from Eligha's mind and over the following days he totally forgot about the entire encounter that had occurred with the older gentleman at the restaurant. As a point of clarification, it is important to note at this point that Eligha had local licenses for his construction business. What this means is that he was not registered and licensed by the state authorities, rather he was a registered only as a local residential contractor with the county. This applied to his masonry contractor license as well.

A short while after the fateful encounter at the restaurant, one day out of the blue, Eligha received a call from one of the county's building officials. Previously, Eligha had a customer who had been unhappy. She desired to have her contractor on site at her job every day. That was not something that Eligha could do because of the number of projects he had going at the time. Eligha and his customer agreed that they would cancel their contract in the middle of the job. She would get another contractor and both parties mutually agreed to move on. Which they did. The county official on the other end of the phone stated that there was a problem with one of Eligha's customers, the lady just mentioned above, explaining further that there was a $500 construction lien left on the customer's property based on work Eligha had done.

That day Eligha immediately called his attorney and got advice on how to handle the lien situation. The attorney he called was the same attorney he had used for his divorce because he did not know a lot of attorneys at the time. His attorney advised him to pay the lien immediately, contact the customer and let her know the lien had been cleared, and to go a step further and get a written acknowledgement and release from the client that showed the lien had been settled. Over the next forty-eight hours Eligha followed the advice of his attorney to the letter. He paid the lien, contacted his customer, and got her written acknowledgement that the lien had been cleared and he took all his documentation to the county's office.

Because he had done exactly what he was told to do by his attorney Eligha thought the incident was over and settled once he turned in the evidence of clearing the lien to the county officials. When he left the county's office, the officials told him everything was cleared up and everything related to the lien had been satisfied. Eligha left the county office that day confident the situation had been handled correctly because he had followed his attorney's advice and he had the word of the people at the county office that everything had been cleared up.

A few days later, Eligha received another phone call from the county saying they needed him to please come in and to bring all his building contracts into the office for review because the county was placing his contractor's license on probation pending an investigation. The county officials took it another step further, they placed the entire incident and investigation in the local newspaper with the article headline stating that **Pryor Homes' contractor's license is suspended until further notice** even though the underlying lien situation had been satisfied.[4]

Having both his name and the company name splashed all over the local newspaper in such a negative fashion had a dramatically tragic impact on Eligha's business and began to take a toll on Eligha personally. In fact, after the article

---

[4] Eligha recalls at that time the local newspaper had been using only black and white photos up until the time his article was published. When the article stating his contractor's license had been suspended ran, it was published with the accompanying photograph of Eligha printed in full color.

ran in the local paper, the once busy and bustling Pryor Homes model home center never received another visitor through its doors again and eventually had to be shut down.

At this point in time, Eligha was not aware of the social and political dynamics that were at play in his situation. In fact, he had totally forgotten about the encounter he had had with the older white developer when he and his fiancé were out to dinner months earlier. Sharing his predicament with people in the community helped to shed some light on the potential forces at play. Meeting with some community leaders he was directed toward the local NAACP chapter, and the local NAACP listened to his story and sided with him and his cause offering to help challenge what appeared to be a full-frontal assault from what Eligha came to know was referred to as the "old boys network"[5] in their county. It was becoming readily apparent that the local forces were lining up against Eligha and were intent on humbling him and hurting his business. Remember the words of the older white developer from that night at dinner, he said, "you will never make another million dollars in this town."

County officials desired to see all his business contracts with the unspoken purpose of seeking to determine his total business revenues and overall personal net worth. Eventually, the county set a hearing date regarding the temporary suspension of Eligha's residential contractor's

---

[5] An **old boys network** is an informal system of support and friendship through which men use their positions of influence to help others who went to the same school or college as they did or who share a similar social background. In our case the commonality was their social status as affluent white men.

license. Once again, Eligha reached out to and retained the same lawyer who had handled his previous divorce case since this was the only attorney with whom he had a working relationship. What Eligha did not know at that time was that his attorney was also employed as the county's attorney as well. It would seem to reason that Eligha's attorney should have disclosed the potential conflict of interest, but no disclosure was ever made.

On the day of the hearing Eligha went out of his way to make a show of confidence and power. He hired a chauffeur for the day to drive him in his Mercedes Benz. He also showed up to court with a bevy of satisfied customers in tow ready to testify on his behalf as well as a representative from the local NAACP chapter. Eligha immediately noticed that two of the local television stations were also in attendance.

As he approached the table near the front where "his attorney" was seated his attorney leaned to him and said, "they have already made up their minds." Eligha said to him, that is okay because we are here and have plenty of testimony and the truth shall set us free. The meeting began and the County Board stated that they have decided to revoke Eligha Pryor's county residential contractor's license and asked if there was anything that needed to be said from the Pryor side. At this point Eligha's attorney stood up and said, "no further questions."

Immediately, the gavel slammed down ending the issue and in less than thirty seconds Eligha had lost his license as a residential contactor. The fact that Eligha had all these witnesses present and ready to support him became irrelevant because his attorney needed to call the witnesses to make them a part of the proceeding. And as Eligha now knows his attorney was in on the plot to take his license, there was no chance the attorney was going to facilitate hearing the witnesses that would have potentially changed the entire outcome.

Shocked by the decision, Eligha immediately broke into tears just as the local television cameras were rolling and focused on him when a reporter asked, "Mr. Pryor, now that your contractor's license has been revoked what are you going to do now?" Eligha looked into the cameras and overcome by the shock and embarrassment he was feeling in the moment he told them a bold face lie. "I am going to retire. I have three chicken restaurants in Gainesville. I am going to retire and run my chicken restaurants." Eligha then jumped into his Mercedes Benz and drove away. The only problem was Eligha did not own any restaurants in Gainesville or anywhere else for that matter. He had no plan and was uncertain as to what he was about to do with his life.

The parameters of the decision by the county to revoke Eligha's license would have allowed Eligha to complete the existing contracts and homes he was currently building. However, completely crushed and unsure of what and how things had just gone down with his license, Eligha was scared that if he continued to work the powers that be would find another way to hurt him and his family. Not willing to take a chance on something else bad occurring, Eligha reached out to the young man, who was also a white man, the same young man that had helped him learn and master the CAD program years earlier. Since the young white gentleman had recently himself been licensed as a residential contractor in the county Eligha simply gave him all his existing contracts no strings attached. The total amount of the contracts Eligha had under construction at the time was well more than $5.5 million dollars and he gave it all away and walked away from the only business he had known since he was a small child.

After taking a little time to recover and gather himself and needing to generate income Eligha made the decision to go back to what he knew best, working as a masonry contractor. So, he took his fancy general contractor's truck and he loaded it up with the tools and gear to once again tackle masonry jobs not as a general contractor but now as a front-line laborer. Eligha thought this was the lowest point he had reached in his life. He had lost everything, his name, his business, the respect of his children and he was back to where he started when he was a little boy and young man, laying block as a masonry contractor. He reactivated his masonry contractor's license which had not been impacted by the whole episode. He went a step further and changed the name of his business from Eligha Pryor Masonry to ENS Enterprises because the new business name had no connection back to his own name and personal brand. No one in the area would give him any jobs, not even to do simple block work. Consequently, no one in any of the surrounding towns would do business with him because of the negative press in the newspaper.

Because his name and reputation had been so damaged in his hometown and local community, he decided to drive approximately 3 hours away to the city of Orlando and he took on a sub-contracted masonry job. Things were going well for just a few weeks when somehow, someway the news of the events in his hometown made their way to the folks in Orlando as well. Eligha lost the gig in Orlando and as a result he decided that with no way to sustain work he was going to have to let his employees go and close the business. And that is exactly what he did.

Eligha had never worked for anyone other than his father when he was young man. For the first time in his life, he struck out and got a job working for someone else who was building a 13-story hotel. He went to work for the first week laying block 13 stories in the air. After his first full week on the job, he received his first paycheck for $352. Eligha thought to himself this is not going to work, he had worked all week, 13 stories in the air and he only made $352. That was his first and last week working on the hotel project.

Even though times were tough and Eligha had no permanent job he never sat still or simply sat at home. Every day he would get up early as he had done his whole life, he would gather up his tools and drive around the outskirts of the surrounding areas approximately 90 miles or so from his home and look for folks who were laying bricks or blocks.

He would pull up to the job and yell at the foreman, are you looking for a good man? Often, simply based on looking at him and his massive frame and seeing he had his tools in hand the foreman would give him a chance and in short order Eligha would demonstrate his skills and the crew would stop laying blocks themselves, put down their trowels and begin to support Eligha setting up his work and watching in amazement at this speed and skill.

When you are not regularly earning money, your savings can go fast and Eligha was no exception. Soon he was receiving calls from debt collectors as the bills mounted. Suppliers of his closed business who had not been paid file lawsuits and Eligha was beginning to be served on a regular basis with the associated paperwork. When one of the process servers was delivering the papers notifying him of another lawsuit Eligha curiously inquired, how much do you get paid for serving these papers to me? Surprised by the answer Eligha decided to become a process server himself and he started the process to get licensed as a process server. After being licensed as a process server, and still facing multiple lawsuits himself, he started serving papers on other people to earn a living for himself.

Taking a full account of his circumstances, Eligha determined he had to make some dramatic changes particularly to his lifestyle. One of the moves he decided to make was to return his Mercedes Benz to the dealer where he had purchased the vehicle. Eligha drove the car to the dealership, parked it on the lot and went inside. He walked up to the salesperson's desk who had sold him the car and dropped the car keys down on the desk. A bit shocked and confused the salesman looked up and asked, "What are you doing Mr. Pryor?"

Eligha told him, "Listen, I can't afford to make the payments on this car anymore, so I am saving us all the trouble and bringing it back to you, so you don't have to come looking for it." The salesman protested and said, "that is not how it works, that is not how we do it." But Eligha left the keys sitting on the salesman's desk and walk out the dealership leaving his Mercedes parked on the lot right where it stood.

To address the debts and lawsuits that were piling up Eligha made another move to seek relief from the growing financial pressures. Eligha met with an attorney who recommended that the best course of action was to file for bankruptcy. Filing for bankruptcy put an end to the lawsuits and mounting collection efforts. As a part of the bankruptcy proceedings the court established a manageable plan that drastically reduced the financial pressures Eligha was under. This decision created a great deal of stress relief and provided more stability to Eligha and his family.

Just as Eligha felt a bit of solid ground under his feet, that August he received a phone call from his mother, she sounded serious in her tone and said, we need to talk. He didn't know what was coming but this call was going to change everything.

Chapter 3

News About Your Father

You can't do it without God:
Your Higher Power is everything.

~ E.P.

One morning Eligha's phone rang. It was Eligha's mom was on the phone, and she sounded concerned, she said, "your dad is sick, I think he has the 'bug' or something." Eligha's life had hit a new low at this point in time. He had lost his name and reputation in the local and surrounding communities. His kids had lost faith in him. He was not employed. Eligha had recently filed for bankruptcy and he was dead broke when his mother called with the news of his father's mystery illness. He was personally at an all-time low.

Together they took his dad to several different local doctors and hospitals and all the tests that were run came back clear not showing any problems, but his father's weight loss was so severe the family knew there was something wrong. After visiting their local doctors and not finding any helpful answers, the family contacted the Mayo Clinic in Jacksonville, Florida to see if they could help identify what was causing the illness and extreme loss of weight his father was experiencing. After some back and forth with the Mayo Clinic over acceptance of his dad's insurance card, the Mayo Clinic finally accepted his dad's insurance card and Eligha's father was cleared to enter the clinic for an examination.

The doctors at the Mayo Clinic did a thorough examination of Eligha's father and discovered that he had stage four cancer, Hodgkin's lymphoma. Hodgkin's lymphoma — formerly known as Hodgkin's disease — is a cancer of the lymphatic system, which is part of your immune system. It may affect people of any age but is most common in people between 20 and 40 years old and those over 55. In Hodgkin's lymphoma, cells in the lymphatic system grow abnormally and may spread beyond it. In Eligha's dad, the cancer was all over his body at this point, in addition to being in his lymphatic system it had spread to his bones and his brain so severely that the doctors at the Mayo gave his father only 20 days to live.

This news simply blew Eligha's mind, how is this possible – how can his hero be sick? For Eligha it was a complete game changer, it was not the loss of his name, his business, nor the loss of all his money, his father had been his hero his whole life and now the doctors were saying his hero was in the last stages of cancer and only had 20 days to live. Eligha was completely devasted. From a spiritual standpoint, Eligha had nowhere to turn at this critical low point in his life. He knew about God, but he never truly believed in God. He was raised to go to church and had regularly attended starting when he was 13 years old with his dad, yet he had always thought God was simply a joke.

Eligha would say at this point in his life he simply did not know God and had never developed a personal relationship with God. As the doctor at the Mayo Clinic laid it all out for his father Eligha had little faith in what his father told the doctor that day. His father, who was then a deacon at his home church, look directly into the doctor's eyes and said, "I believe God is going to heal me."

The doctors scheduled Eligha's dad for surgery the next day and placed two ports, one in his head and one in his chest. With the ports in place an aggressive battery of chemotherapy was started and Eligha watched as his dad prayed for God to heal him and went through the prescribed treatments. Something changed for Eligha when his father fell ill, and it happened almost in an instant. As Eligha watched his lifelong hero battle for his life Eligha's own heart softened.

When you must watch a loved-one suffering with something you cannot control, when there is nothing you can do to assist them, it has an effect on your whole being. Eligha was no different. Prior to his business downfall Eligha had been the man, not only to himself, but he had earned the respect and admiration of his father as well. Not so long ago, his father would listen to him about business and finances and now with only weeks to live, according to the doctors, his father was witnessing his son at an all-time low point. In a word it was humbling for Eligha, he was humbled by the enormity of it all.

Eligha stayed by his father's side over the following weeks and each time they returned to visit the doctor for check-ups the doctor would continuously say the same thing, "this is unbelievable." The cancer was going backward, the tests and reports would say. Three weeks went by, more than the twenty days the doctors had predicted and with each visit the results were the same, the cancer is not growing, in fact, the cancer is receding, the tumors were getting smaller in response to his dad's treatment.

Over the next three months the doctors were all amazed at the rate of his father's recovery. It was miraculous to say the least. The cancer was still there, but the treatments were working according to the doctors. The good reports from the doctors led to the change of heart for Eligha. He was thankful to have his dad with him still. It took a long while, eight years to be exact, but Eligha's father made a complete recovery, his cancer went into full remission and all his doctors could say was, "unbelievable."

With every day, with every report of improvement from his dad's doctors Eligha was starting to believe that there must be a God somewhere because his dad was supposed to be dead in twenty days and the chemo was helping his dad heal. So, from that point on Eligha started wanting to get to know God. Who and how was it that his father was being saved? He had to know. He had to know more about this God that had saved his hero, who was this God that gave him his father back?

At this time Eligha was still broke. But this experience made it clear to him that insurance was very important. Eligha wanted to get for himself the same kind of protection his dad had. He reached out to an insurance agent saying to her, "I need insurance. Until this experience with my dad, I didn't know the importance having an insurance card."

Eligha knew full well that if his dad had not had an insurance card, he would not have been able to go to the Mayo Clinic. If he had not gone to the Mayo Clinic, he would not be alive today. The insurance agent was knowledgeable, and she helped Eligha get a health insurance policy at a low and reasonable cost. She also planted a seed in Eligha's mind when she shared, "You have a great personality, you should become an insurance agent yourself."

Her words resonated with Eligha, and he thought to himself, me, the insurance guy, that is it. As the insurance guy, Eligha realized, he could help people be in the same situation as his dad, in the position to have an insurance card in case of a health care emergency. He now knew first-hand how important this was. With a new heart centered on helping people as a way to say, thank you to God for saving his father, Eligha set out to get his insurance license and he began to sell insurance.

Keep in mind all of this occurred before congress passed the Affordable Care Act (ACA), also known as

Obamacare, so there were millions of Americans who were not covered by employer sponsored health care plans at this time. Once he got his insurance license Eligha went into underserved communities, areas where people did not typically come to sell insurance. He desired to help his customers not just sell them something.

Initially, he joined a national insurance company and got to work. But this new company was driven by selling people products not helping people improve their lives. The company's philosophy of profits over people did not align with Eligha's new people-centered heart and focus. After one month he decided to leave that company and searched for a new company that aligned more closely with his own vision of helping others.

In short order, he found an excellent company that had nationwide offices and he joined their sales team. Over the next two years, his favor showed bright as he worked his way to becoming the number two salesperson in the entire country for his new company. His success was rewarded as he was able to make over $2.0 million in only his second year in the business plus he had no overhead.

It was clear to see that Eligha had changed on the inside. He used to only drive fancy and expensive cars. Once he was again earning at such a high level, cars and showing off were no longer important to him. He drove a regular car. He still only wanted to be able to help others as a way of saying thank you to God for saving his father two years earlier. Eligha came to know he not only had God in his corner, but he had God's favor. He had been covered by God's favor all his life even when he did not understand what he had.

In his younger years he thrived and bathed in his own success and when folks like his father adulated and congratulated him, Eligha took all the credit. He would exclaim, "I'm the man" feeling he was solely responsible for his success and triumphs in life. Having been transformed by his father's ordeal, Eligha now knew the source of his favor and good fortune. He knew it all resides with God. He was gifted strength by God at birth. God empowered him to learn his craft from some of the best laborers on the planet before he was even eight years old. God made him the fastest mason in the world. It was all God's favor and blessings.

Chapter 4

One Of The Fastest Masons In The World

> *Jesus said to them, "Have you never read in the Scriptures: 'The stone the builders rejected has become the cornerstone; the Lord has done this, and it is marvelous in our eyes'?"*
>
> Matthew 21:42 (NIV)

As long as he can remember, far back into his childhood, Eligha has been surrounded by the art of masonry, influenced by his father, and learning from his father's business. In fact, one of Elijah's natural gifts is laying concrete block. At an early age he set it clearly in his mind that he was going to be a mason like his dad. Born with a competitive spirit, Eligha's goal was not to simply be a mason, his desire was to be one of the best mason's to ever touch a cement block. And in no uncertain terms he accomplished this goal with a high degree of gusto infused with skilled determination.

To give some perspective on the craft of laying concrete block, each 8" x 16" concrete block weighs 35 pounds apiece. The average skilled mason will lay an average of 250-300 of these blocks in any given day. That would be considered a good day's work. On an exceptionally good day one might be able to finish laying upwards of 500 blocks during a normal 8-hour shift.

When someone has a 500-block day, it typically is when, in the business what they call, "running wall." When running wall, you typically are working in a straight line with no leads, no corners, and it often does not include any windows or other complicating features. When someone comes in with a 500-block day it is a big deal. They are not going to be able to give this kind of performance every day, but some days their work will be special.

Eligha treated laying block as if it were his sport, he approached it in the same manner that he had approached playing football when he was young. When he played football, he was a tenacious competitor, and he brought the same intensity and dedication to his work as a mason. Like any person completely dedicated to their sport he gave it his all and with every day he worked diligently to add to his skills and to improve his performance level in every facet of the endeavor.

Additionally, the strength and conditioning work he performed in preparation to play football were directly transferrable skills to the task of laying block. Precisely placing a large thirty-five-pound block of cement requires a great deal of strength and endurance. Mental focus and sustained attention to detail are each both critical components to keeping each block perfectly in the desired location, especially when moving at a high rate of speed.

On his best day Elijah was able to lay 3,800 blocks in one 8-hour shift. That is more than 7.5 times better than what most would consider an exceptional day. This is because Eligha treated it like a sport. Technique, it is all about technique when laying block. And Eligha was not simply running wall, he laid the block for an entire building that was to become a medical center. He laid 3,800 blocks and it included everything: doors, openings, covered openings everything that was present in the entire building's plans. On that day Eligha had 11 laborers feeding him materials to keep up with his pace of work.

To understand the magnitude and significance of Eligha's skills as a block mason it requires you to visualize the process itself. When there is a fresh footer that has been laid the first aspect to getting your job perfect is to have your mortar (mud) mixed properly so that it has the right consistency. This is important because if the mud is not the right consistency, then it will not be able to set up and hold the block once the block is laid on top of it. Once your mud is ready then you start to spread it in the area where you are going to start laying your block. So, in this case you would start to place a nice amount of mud onto your trowel and then spread it on the footer and perhaps a little on the first block you are about to lay down.

When the first block is laid down into the mud you must level the block. Leveling the block means it is set perfectly in term of going up or down on a horizontal plane. If the block is not level, you use the handle of your trowel to tap the block down into the mud until it lines up perfectly level. Tap, tap here. Perhaps a little tap, tap there until it lines up perfectly. Next you need to make sure the first block is plum as well. Plum refers to lining up left or right on the vertical plane. Same process applies, using your sight line if any part of the block is not perfectly plum you use the handle of the trowel to tap the block into place. Tap, tap. Tap, tap.

Getting the first block perfectly level and plum is of critical importance because it will set the tone for the rest of the blocks that are going to be set on that line of blocks. After that first block is set correctly and to your satisfaction, when you are doing a standard lead, (a lead is a corner), you would go four blocks in one direction and once you get them all leveled and plum, you set four and a half blocks in the other direction at a precise 90-degree angle. When you lay your first corner that is where you are going to pull your string off in order to lay down the first level of your wall.

The corner is the most important thing to your wall because if your lead is incorrect, then your whole wall is going to end up incorrect as well. Likewise, if your corner is not plum, there is no way that your entire wall will end up plum. So, your lead must be perfect from the start. Normally, it takes your average mason about 45 minutes to an hour to build an eight-course lead. Eligha can perfectly set up an eight-course lead in about ten minutes.

Whatever you do on the first row or course of block sets up what will happen on each row of block that you add above it. If your first course is perfect, the second course can also be laid and tapped into place to be level and plum.

Around his hometown, Eligha was known to be the best mason around. People would wait two to three weeks for him to be available, not solely for his speed on a job, but also for the quality of the work once he was done. They knew that if Eligha laid the blocks on the job, the finished product was going to be perfect. If someone else could get to the job sooner, they would wait for Eligha because they knew he was going to deliver a perfect result. Eligha had the mason game on lock because he had mastered the craft.

Eligha was told if he stayed in his lane as a mason, he would have never had any problems in his hometown. Builders had no problem with him being their subordinate, or sub-contractor. If folks could call him to work on their job, there was no problem. Had he refused to grow his business capacity and stayed in his place or his lane as they say, there would have been no attempt to bring about his downfall. It was when Eligha sought to grow and become the builder, to become licensed as the general contractor, that is when he encountered a problem in the community.

Almost all of life equates to the art of laying blocks. Each event and task build on the prior events and work in one's journey. Care must be taken to lay a solid foundation, one that is strong and level. You need a foundation that is able to support the weight and strain of subsequent experiences to come.

Every experience or event equates to a block in our walls of life. The act of reflection and self-evaluation provides the opportunity to tap our recent blocks into place to make the new blocks level and plum. This tapping of our blocks can take many forms and result in a number of different corrective opportunities. Sometimes we may need to return to an individual to offer an apology or make amends in order to tap the past situation back into alignment.

We may need to make a life course adjustment to realign ourselves with our desired goal or destination. Perhaps we see our wall is not lining up with our goals and it requires that we make a change to our job or employer because our current situation does not align with our values or principles. It could be that you envision something different for yourself and you need to tap, tap, tap, tap a new path for a better work-life balance, a more fulfilling use of your day, or simply for better pay.

Too many people float through life without having a written set of plans to guide them. They are building their life's wall without checking for alignment and accurate block placement. Imagine for a moment what would happen if a construction crew were to attempt to build a structure without plans to guide their work. What would the resulting structure look like? Do you think it would be a harmonious and happy work site?

Now consider how this same example applies to your own life journey and the virtual wall we build one experience or block at a time. After his father's illness and miraculous recovery, Eligha started building a fresh foundation infused with his newfound faith and belief in a higher power of God. He chose to build a spiritual foundation. While laying down his freshly poured foundation, he started drafting plans for his life that focused on being grateful for all the blessings God had given him. His goal was to help others and place the people he encountered in need of assistance as his priority.

He would regularly check his work and actions to make sure everything was going according to plan. The same way he would do it if he was physically laying blocks for a building, checking often to make sure his labor matches the architectural plans for the project.

You can follow this example. If necessary, you can call a time-out and choose to create a freshly poured foundation for yourself. You can choose to tap into a higher power. No matter what you choose you must have a plan and like building a perfectly level and plum wall, you must check your progress regularly to ensure you are on the right track and still operating according to your plans. Like most aspects of life, the people you have assisting you and supporting you with your work are critically important. And the most crucial person in your life is your life-partner or spouse.

Chapter 5

Don't Forget Where You Come From

"My father has always been my hero. He taught all of us kids to believe in ourselves and showed us that anything was possible. With a 5th grade education, he built a successful business and always provided for his family."

~ E.P.

From his early childhood for as long as he could remember Eligha idolized his father and always considered his dad to be his personal hero. His dad, Eligha Sr., was born in 1945, the second oldest child, eventually having 13 siblings for a total of 14 kids all together. His dad's mom got married when she was only 12 years old, and his dad's father was almost 30 at the time. She was only 15 years old when she had Eligha's dad.

Eligha's dad eventually had nine brothers and four sisters. When he was born in 1945 in Augusta, Arkansas it was a small integrated farming community of less than 1,500 people 75 miles northeast of Little Rock located on the east bank of the White River. Eligha's grandparents were sharecroppers who lived in a small two-bedroom wood-framed house that was owned by the white man who owned the fields where almost everyone worked, including his father. The house had no bathroom, there was an outhouse, a kitchen, and a living room. Their parents slept in one bedroom, all ten of the boys slept together in the other bedroom and the four girls slept in the living room.

Eligha's father remembers that as kids they each only received two pair of jeans and one pair of shoes per year. This may seem like a meager allotment per person, but once all the children were born keep in mind that amounts to 28 pairs of jeans and 14 pairs of shoes each year. Not to mention undergarments, etc. All together 14 children need a whole lot of clothes.

When they played outside, they played barefoot because they only had the one pair of shoes and could not afford for them to get worn down simply from playing around. If one of the children cut their foot while playing their mother would administer a home remedy which included cleaning the cut with kerosine as the disinfectant. Because he was the second oldest child, he had a lot of responsibility with regards to his younger brothers and sisters. Eligha's father came out of school and started taking care of his younger brothers and sisters and working in the fields with his daddy somewhere around 5th or 6th grade. He says that on the first day of school one year his mother sent him to the schoolhouse and when he came home, she said, "good you got your books, so you can use them to study here at home because you are not going back."

Even with 16 mouths to feed the family always had enough food to eat. The family grew their own vegetables, they had fruit trees in their yard, and they raised chickens and hogs. When the fruit was ripe on the trees the kids would pick it right from the tree or grab them off the ground right after they fell. Eligha's grandmother would spend weeks in the fall cooking and canning all the extra fruits and vegetables so the family would have food throughout the year.

There's a common family story shared about how daddy would go out into the yard and grab up one of the chickens expertly ringing the fowl's neck and delivering the bird to mother so she could clean and prep it. Mom would have a huge pot of water boiling and she would add veggies, the chicken, and a bunch of homemade dumplings. When it was finished the whole family would feast on the meal of mom's scrumptious chicken and dumplings.

Although they were sharecroppers and earned very little in actual wages their father still had a car. Eligha's father always shares that his Daddy was the hardest working man that he ever knew. He learned his work ethic from watching both his parents working on the farm especially his father. His father was one of the fastest workers on the farm. He could outwork two or three other fieldhands. In addition to his work ethic, his father was also said to have been a pretty good dancer, known to cut a rug at the local night spot near the farm in Augusta.

A favorite childhood memory often recounted by Eligha's Dad is the Christmas when the kids received a little red wagon as a gift. They would take turns pulling each other in that wagon. The kids played endlessly with the wagon riding it until literally the wheels fell off. His dad laughs and says when the wheels came off, we turned it into a sled and kept the fun going. Life was simple, required lots of continuous work on the farm in Augusta, but the Pryor clan was a happy, close knit and fun-loving family.

At the age of 15 Eligha's father left Augusta after a bus came through town one day and offered to take him to Florida where they said, "money grows on trees." It turns out that the money they were referring to was for picking grapefruits and oranges off the trees in Florida. Reflecting on his own life's journey, Eligha's dad says, "if you put God first, things will work out for you. Back in the day we believed in prayer. We regularly used the vehicle and power of prayer."

Eligha's dad has always wanted his children to have more than he did. His dad's desire was for his children to have a greater opportunity than he did back in Augusta, Arkansas. His dream was for his kids to have the opportunity to get a college education since he felt that would be a game changer in their lives. Although college was not Eligha's path, his father was overwhelmed with pride in how Eligha excelled as both a mason and a general contractor and later as the insurance guy glowing in the knowledge that his son had achieved a level of accomplishment and success measures beyond his own while building upon the craft he had taught and embedded in his son.

Remember at the start of Eligha's story when he was standing in the closet of his mansion preparing for dinner with his fiancé, he had not yet had any life experiences or received any instructions on how both racism and envy can enter the equation. The first thirty years of his life sheltered him from these realities and had unfolded in such a way that he just did not know how these dynamics were at play in the world.

The circumstances in his hometown that led to him losing his contractor's license gave him a crash course on the motivations of some men and the power and influence of the good old boys network in a small southern community. Even though Eligha's father grew up during the Jim Crow era[6] in rural Arkansas as the son of a sharecropper, Eligha himself was never fully conscious of America's racial issues because his father never shared or focused on this aspect of life.

The way Eligha was raised by his dad, he wasn't raised where he regularly heard or was taught 'that the white man this and the black man that.' Growing up as a child there

---

[6] **Jim Crow laws** were state and local laws that enforced racial segregation in the Southern United States and elsewhere within the United States. These laws were enacted in the late 19th and early 20th centuries by white Southern Democrat-dominated state legislatures to disenfranchise and remove political and economic gains made by black people during the Reconstruction period. Jim Crow laws were enforced until 1965.

was never any references to 'because of the white man I can't this or I can't do that.' Eligha's parents did not raise him like that. Even though these things were going on, Eligha was not raised to focus on or to pay attention to things like that, it was never shared with him. Eligha's daddy always told and showed him that anything was possible.

Eligha's dad did not raise his children to be afraid of anything. They were not to allow man made obstacles to prevent them from becoming strong and capable adults. It was all about, if you want it, you go get it. You work hard for it. People have made the way and given you the opportunity, so if you work hard, you can reap the benefits because of your labor. Because Eligha was raised like this, he took things like earthy success for granted. He also took the mindset his daddy gave his kids for granted, too. Now, knowing how others think and feel out in the world, Eligha has learned to keep many things to himself, play his cards closer to his chest, and to be humbler.

But these new understandings and awareness about life and its harsh realities came with a downside. After the experience of losing his license, Eligha developed and harbored a serious mistrust of white people, especially older white men. Like so many who are injured and hurt, Eligha not only did not trust white people, and he was vocal about his distrust. Now, he would drop negatively charged comments to the tune of, "the white man this and the white man that." But we are all God's children, and Eligha was about to learn it is not the skin color of the man that determines his value and worth it is the heart of the man that counts.

This mindset was directly challenged when Eligha met an older white man Mr Harris. When Eligha met Mr. Harris, he had no trust for white men and Mr. Harris was an older white man on top of it. Just like the older white developer who had precipitated his downfall. But Mr. Harris practiced looking at a man's heart and judging folks on the content of their character. Mr. Harris not only saw Eligha's work ethic and recognized his skills as a craftsman, but he also observed that Eligha was about helping other people and Mr. Harris began to cultivate a relationship. Their relationship grew from a single business transaction into one of friendship and then into a full-blown business collaboration with Mr. Harris becoming Eligha's financial backer as he sought to take on a new assignment he received directly from God.

Chapter 6

Support Systems, Mentors & the Importance of Mentorship

Support Systems:

The Right Life Partner Makes All The Difference

Be completely humble and gentle; be patient, bearing with one another in love. Make every effort to keep the unity of the Spirit through the bond of peace.

Ephesians 4:2-3 (NIV)

Who you choose as your spouse, mate, or life partner can make all the difference in the trajectory of your life's path. Your chosen mate will either support you and propel you forward, or they will limit your growth and hold you back from living the life of your dreams. As we discussed earlier in this book, Eligha made a less than ideal choice when picking his first wife, which resulted in a contentious divorce, and led to him making a show of building a house that, in his heart, he did not want to build. In a twist of circumstance, in the aftermath of this initial poor decision, Eligha was able to meet the mate that would be there for him through thick and thin.

When sharing a love story, it is always appreciated and often best to simply start at the beginning of the tale. So let's start at the beginning and let me share with you how Eligha initially met his wife. Right before the two met, the lady that would later become his wife had recently experienced a divorce. Through the twists and turns of life and the divine plan laid out by the Creator, Eligha and his wife-to-be were introduced through a series of conversations and efforts by both of their fathers. You see, their fathers had been friends for years and knew each other well for a long time. The introduction made by their fathers was not intended to be a romantic match making exercise, rather it was intended as a business meeting between the two. But when people meet, sometimes sparks fly, eyes are opened to possibility and a new path is forged.

Eligha was impressed with the lady his dad asked him to meet; she was beautiful, a high-class lady, and a banker with a big-time job in a bank. This darling of a lady needed a contractor to assist her with building a new home and she was crystal clear on what she wanted in her new house.

Although surprised by the age of the building contractor her dad had recommended, the lady was impressed with the man and his mannerisms. She showed Eligha the blueprints of the home she wanted, and they discussed the particulars of the building project. Eligha made enough of an impression in their meetings that she gave him the contract to build her new home. It was a magnificent home in both scale and grandeur, a big building project for any contractor, to be clear. Once engaged, Eligha and his crew did the work in a professional and, more importantly, in a timely and efficient manner. The home, Eligha's first complete home as a general contractor, was completed in just under three months.

His beautiful and intelligent new client was so impressed with the speed and quality of the work Eligha had performed in completing her new home that she invited Eligha out to lunch and the two commenced a burgeoning friendship. This is how Eligha and wife-to-be initially became friends. As time went on, the friendship flourished and grew into something more. As Eligha likes to put it, "the new client" became "his girl."

Over time, Eligha went from completing his first home as a contractor to being on the top of his game in the building world. All the while he had an amazing partner by his side as he made his accent. She was there for him, and she stayed by his side when he lost everything. She knew the kind of man that she had, that he was a determined person and she trusted and was committed to him. Eligha had the big home he built for himself after his divorce and she had the home that Eligha had built for her when they first met.

Once Eligha's troubles commenced in his hometown that led to his downfall, it was difficult for him to express himself and share the important details of the financial troubles he was facing with his lady. Eligha was not used to sharing on this level with the woman in his life and he also had never faced circumstances such as these at any point before in his life. One day when she came home from work, she discovered their new family no longer lived in the big house and before leaving for work that morning she had no idea of what was coming in terms of the move.

When his lady left for work that morning, Eligha had a crew of his guys show up soon after she left, and load up a U-Haul truck. The crew moved the family from the big house that they owned into another big house that Eligha had rented in an attempt not to compromise their lifestyle. The loss of his business and major hit to his brand led to a complete loss of almost everything at the time. Once he was forced to close his business from a lack of available work due to the bad press and the local rumor mill, Eligha eventually had to declare bankruptcy.

She never put Eligha through anything with regards to his financial troubles. Eligha had to study and had to get new licenses to get things into place to relaunch his new careers. Eligha was worried about losing this amazing lady and his new family because of all the changes they were going through. But she supported him through all the bad times. She didn't require that they go out and have fancy dinners. She just sat back, re-grouped and was a supportive wife. One-month Eligha fell into a situation where he was not able to pay the rent and she stepped up and paid the rent which amounted to about two-thousand dollars.

Eligha says that event killed him because he was not able to support the family and take care of the home. The next month Eligha sold all his jewelry so his wife never had to cover the expenses for the family again. Eligha shares that he feels like less than a man when he is not able to take care of his home.

> *"My wife was a perfect person in my life to allow me to focus and grind without putting me under any kind of pressure to get back on top. She said she believed in me, and she told me she knew I was going to be OK. She always told me, 'You're going to be OK.'*
>
> *And she was right, I came out OK. That's why she gets anything she wants. This mansion I built, I built it for my wife. This big ole house doesn't mean nothing to me. I built this crib for her, this is just a house, but she makes it a home. I built this big house in appreciation of her being such a good woman."*
>
> ~ E.P. being overhead talking about his wife

Bottomline, the right choice of who will be your spouse makes all the difference. Eligha recalls that he was eager to come home at night. He was not out in the streets, hanging out in nightclubs or bars. This woman he had chosen to settle down with made his house a home and more importantly she supported and uplifted him in all that he attempted to do in redefining himself and rebuilding his life. Her continuous encouragement that he was going to be okay, without pressure or demand gave him the space to replant himself, to re-educate himself, and to build something meaningful.

Eventually, she would transition from her job at the bank and become a major contributor to the business that Eligha rebuilt from the ground up. Acting as his office manager and confidant she now keeps the trains running on time and the books in perfect order. The home the family now occupies is her castle and each appointment and detail springs from her vision and exceptional attention to detail. There is no doubt that it is Eligha's business, but like a car, or a powerful jet plane, it is the engine, underneath the hood, behind the scenes if you will, that makes the whole thing move.

Be mindful of who you place in the all-important position of being your life's co-pilot. When there is a crisis, you need a person by your side who makes the most horrific situation more tolerable; someone who can be your peace and calm in the midst of a rising storm. Take an inventory, if the person you are with brings drama and heartache, you may seriously need to reassess their role. Would they stay with you through a down-size? Are they only interested in the lobster dinners and the nice cars? There are ups and downs in life and we all need a person by our side who is going to be there in the most extreme of downsides that life has to offer. The co-pilot you chose needs to be encouraging and uplifting in times of doubt and uncertainty.

Everyone deserves the type of partnership and love that Eligha shares with his wife. You deserve it. You need it to be the best you that you can be. If you have that person in your life, value them and let them know as often as you can that they are the lighthouse of your journey. Honor them and do your best to build them as they invest and build you. If your situation is not this type of supportive and loving arrangement, you need to embrace the courage to move on. You need to forge a new path in hopes that the right partner will present themselves and help you to become the most fulfilled and dynamic you possible.

Remember always that you are the captain of your ship. You are ultimately responsible for everything that happens onboard and for everyone you allow to travel with you on the journey.

Mentors help you grow

Mentor

/ˈmenˌtôr,ˈmenˌtər/

noun

noun: **mentor**; plural noun: **mentors**

1. an experienced and trusted adviser or guide.
2. an influential senior sponsor or supporter.

"Find a person who is doing what you want to do and model after them."

~E.P.

The initial path to finding mentorship beyond that of his own father all started about three years into Eligha's insurance journey. One day, one of Eligha's insurance clients came to him and shared a tough situation that the client found himself in. The client had purchased a home some years earlier and found himself in a financial crisis where he was going to lose his home in a foreclosure. The client explained further that he had a wonderful four-bedroom house, and it was more than just a house it was also his family's home.

Instead of losing the home, Eligha's client approached him with a proposition, would Eligha be interested in stepping in and purchasing the home so that that client would not be forced to move. Eligha asked the client what bank held the mortgage on the home and the client explained that a bank did not own the mortgage on the house, it was held by a private individual, a private investor who had built the home and sold it to the client years earlier. The client went on to explain that the investor was an older gentleman and was unusually private in his business affairs and dealings. This pronouncement completely intrigued Eligha because up until this point in time he had never come across any private individuals carrying mortgages on a property. Right then and there Eligha made up his mind that he needed to meet this gentleman and learn more about his business and more importantly, he wanted to add this property to his personal real estate portfolio.

The client went on to share that the investor's name was Mr. Franklin Harris adding that Mr. Harris in addition to being a bit reclusive he had recently suffered a broken hip and the injury may make it more difficult to get the private gentleman to engage in a conversation about the property. On that day the client took Eligha to see Mr. Harris at his office and they both approached Mr. Harris' office door together. They knocked on the door and someone came to the door without opening it. Eligha's client explained through the closed door, "Hello, Mr. Harris, I am here with my insurance guy and his name is Eligha Pryor and he would like to talk to you about buying my house from you." Mr. Harris was polite as shared through the closed door that he had broken his hip and explained that he was not able to meet with the two men. Eligha was determined and now knowing where to find the elusive Mr. Harris made up in his mind that he would return and try again the following week.

One-week later, Eligha returned to the same location and once again he approached the door for a second time knocking politely and waiting patiently. Inside he could tell that Mr. Harris was stirring, but the door remained closed, and no conversation was had on this second attempt just like the initial visit. Eligha knew Mr. Harris was in the office and aware of his attempt to speak with him because he could be seen peeping out of the window to see who was at the door. This second rejection did not dampen the desire Eligha had to meet the private investor and more importantly it only fueled the fire Eligha had burning in his belly to purchase the available property.

Like so many instances of challenge Eligha has faced, he was not going to give up simply because of a closed door. Another week went by and once again Eligha returned to Mr. Harris' place and again he approached and knocked on the door and waited. They often say, the third time is the charm and low and behold three weeks after Eligha and the troubled homeowner first approached the same door with no answer, Mr. Harris opened the door and politely invited Eligha inside. Surprised and excited Eligha entered and both men sat down and engaged in a wonderfully comfortable conversation about the property facing foreclosure. Truth be told, both men were caught off guard with how easy and relatable the flow of this first conversation developed with Eligha sharing his relationship with the defaulting homeowner, bits of his background as a former mason and developer and peppering Mr. Harris with questions about his background and how he came to be a private mortgage holder.

Eligha learned that Mr. Harris was 85 years old at the time they first met. They had a miraculous first encounter that ended with Mr. Harris agreeing to sell the property in question to Eligha. Eligha joyfully recounts how this was the first blessing he received from seeking out and meeting Mr. Harris. Eligha really wanted to acquire this foreclosure property of his client's, but he was also fully aware that at this point in time he could not pursue traditional means of financing since the financial struggles of his downfall were still running at full tilt including the impact of the bankruptcy he had been forced to enter when he lost his license and gave up his business. It also served as an additional fuel to his fire to meet such a non-traditional private lender and investor such as Mr. Harris because he felt in his heart that with Mr. Harris there were new possibilities.

When it came time to negotiate the purchase price of the four-bedroom foreclosure property with a then market value of about $96,000 Mr. Harris asked Eligha, "how much do you want to give me for this foreclosure property?" Eligha responded, "I am at a complete loss, Mr. Harris, I can't put a price on a transaction of this nature." Mr. Harris said in response, "I'll tell you what, you give me $25,000 for this property and the house is yours." Eligha almost not believing the offer, agreed to the deal and recounts that from that point on, his blessing from Mr. Franklin Harris began to flow quite frequently.

With their first meeting and business transaction concluded, Mr. Harris ended by inviting Eligha to join him for lunch in the near future so that they could continue to get to know one another and keep the conversation going, which Eligha agreed to without hesitation. And that is exactly what happened. Eligha and "Mr. Frank," the name Eligha began to adoringly call his new friend, became regular lunch buddies. At the point in time when Eligha first engaged Mr. Harris about buying that first residential foreclosure he was still reeling in his own mind from the past destruction that the local old boy network had wrought on his business, personal life, and his own reputation throughout the community. At the time, he distrusted white people, especially older white men, yet here he was developing a deep fondness for an 85-year-old white man, regularly having lunches together and let it be known, becoming the best of friends with Mr. Frank.

In fact, Mr. Frank was starting to see Eligha not only as a friend but as a special part of his life and would routinely introduce Eligha around town as his son. They began to spend more and more time together with Mr. Frank mentoring and sharing all of his life experiences and learned knowledge and Eligha intently soaking it all up like a sponge. Mr. Frank would invite Eligha to join him at his Rotary Club gatherings, take him to lunches at private clubs where he was a member, always introducing Eligha to those in attendance as his son. Throughout all these wondrous experiences Eligha came to understand in a deep and meaningful way that it is not all about the color of a person. Eligha was being shown that it is all about a person's heart and Mr. Frank himself had a great heart. Mr. Frank could see that Eligha, too, had a wonderful heart and was well-intentioned to help others. This bonded the two men even closer to one another.

Mr. Frank was uncannily open and forward in the sharing of his personal story and their accompanying mentorship lessons. Mr. Frank was born into a wealthy family that owned lots of land somewhere up north and his family at one point in history were slaveholders. As a young child, Mr. Frank formed an opinion in his own young mind that all people deserved to be treated fairly and given a fair chance to excel and succeed in life. When he was a young boy, he shared with Eligha how he would stow away what he called 'good food' from the family's table and sneak off to deliver the food to the workers who toiled to work the family land. When Mr. Frank grew older, but still a young man, his parents both passed away and he inherited their lands and money. He took his inheritance and moved south to Ft. Pierce, Florida where he used his wealth to start to build affordable housing intended for people of color. He built scores of single-family homes and offered these homes with no money down at a low cost often only $25,000 per home.

Learning the personal facts and history behind Mr. Frank's life and his professional endeavors as a developer to help people of color acquire homes they could actually own forced Eligha to re-evaluate his own negative experiences with the white man. Before the events of his downfall Eligha had little life experience or interaction with white men, particularly older white men, and his worldview was not heavily focused on race. The events of his downfall and the fact that the situation was orchestrated and facilitated by the local old boy network had a dramatic impact on his perspective and completely tarnished his opinion and view of white people as a collective whole. Mr. Frank was a real world and purposeful encounter that forced a complete rethinking of Eligha's entire mindset on the issue.

Their relationship developed and grew day by day. Mr. Frank intimately shared how he had built thousands and thousands of homes placing families in each one and yet, he felt utterly alone. His heart ached because he never received any type of communication of appreciation or thanks, not a note or a card expressing any type of gratitude for all the work he had done to build so many communities. This lack of affection and appreciation bothered Mr. Frank a great deal and he spoke on the subject often. It was into this void that Eligha stepped without knowing and Mr. Frank devoured the gift with gusto. Mr. Frank wanted Eligha to go with him everywhere that he went and always shared stories and vignettes about his life while they were together. One of Mr. Frank's favorite topics was fondly remembering his late wife, because Mr. Frank was a widower. One of the pearls of wisdom Mr. Franks often repeated to Eligha like a mantra was, "when you have a wife that supports you, appreciate and adore her for that gift. In return for her loving support, you must give her anything she desires." He would elaborate and emphasize, "do it without question because it is hard to find a woman that will support a man in his endeavors, period."

Eligha himself has observed so many folks who end up in relationships that are more like prisons than paradise. There are lots of men and women who do not support and foster the pursuit of a dream held by their significant other. They are in a sort of bondage because of this lack of support and acceptance. And for this reason alone both Eligha and Mr. Frank both considered themselves extraordinarily lucky that they both found mates who were full supporters of all they ever endeavored to undertake. From the time they were dating Eligha found in his wife a completely supportive and encouraging mate, even in the lowest points of his downfall she constantly echoed that he would be okay and believed he would figure it all out.

An important elemental ingredient in any mentorship relationship is one of trust built on a mutual respect for one another. As the relationship grew between Mr. Frank and Eligha so did their respect and admiration for one another. Mr. Frank would regularly drop actionable pearls of wisdom from his decades of experience as a home developer to assist Eligha in his business development. For example, Mr. Frank shared how when it came to sourcing your workers to help in building a home that it was important to understand simple things like the wages that workers were paid as this would ultimately have a dramatic impact on your bottom line. Due to several factors workers in one county would garner higher wages than workers from neighboring counties although there were negligible skill levels and resulting outputs. For this reason, Mr. Frank would counsel Eligha to pay close attention to details of this nature in his business and look to hire the most cost-effective laborers for a job and not necessarily the closest in terms of geographic location.

Eligha trusted Mr. Frank implicitly and made notes and acted on all the advice that he received from the generous gentleman. When Eligha received a 4:00AM revelation from

God instructing him to return to his hometown and start building affordable housing in the low-income neighborhoods, he took the mission to Mr. Frank. Mr. Frank came onboard as his financial backer for the project. Eligha would identify a building for sale and he and Mr. Frank would partner on the purchase of the building.

Then, unexpectedly in February of 2018 Mr. Frank, at the age of 90, suddenly passed away. It was a tragic loss for Eligha, one he did not expect, because in addition to the heartache and pain at the loss of his friend, he also lost his first mentor. Now, as is often the case, when one door closes another door opens. Or put another way, God did not leave Eligha hanging. Out of the blue, three months prior to Mr. Frank's unexpected passing, Eligha was contacted by a woman who said she was looking to purchase ten residential houses all at once.

The only issue was Eligha did not have ten homes in his available inventory, he only had three homes available to sell at the time. This lady was intent on acquiring the properties in question and she said she would take the three homes that Eligha had available, and the deal was set. The lady's name was Ms. Gwen and Ms. Gwen was all about her business. She made the deal to purchase the three homes that Eligha had available and made arrangements to have the money transferred into escrow the next day. Not only did she purchase the three homes from Eligha, but she quickly fostered a strong belief in Eligha and his business acumen and without missing a beat from the loss of his mentor Mr.

Frank, Ms. Gwen leaped into the void and became Eligha's new mentor.

When observing some of the differences between Ms. Gwen and Mr. Frank, Eligha starts with the obvious, Ms. Gwen is an older white woman in her 80's. As a businessperson she is more outgoing and more aggressive in her approach as compared to the late Mr. Frank. Ms. Gwen represented a new life lesson for Eligha. Building on his reversal on trusting and dealing with people not based solely on their skin color, this older white lady forced Eligha to re-evaluate how he perceived and thought about women and their roles and place in society. Interacting with this older white lady, who is sharp, aggressive in her business, decisive and always positive about life, Eligha learned he could not water down a woman's role or place in life. Ms. Gwen's example makes it impossible for him to continue to do anything like that at all.

Eligha reflects on how as a big ole black dude, raised by a father from the deep south in Arkansas, he is amused to see himself being guided by this little bitty old white lady in business. When Ms. Gwen talks, Eligha listens. Ms. Gwen listens to Eligha as they discuss projects and ideas and she will interject, "Hey don't do that. That won't work." Still, Eligha knows that Ms. Gwen is looking out for his best interests and looking to help him grow as a businessman. Through his relationship with Ms. Gwen, Eligha has learned that he cannot neglect the talents and the gifts of women.

They too have been blessed and favored to create and flourish in the world of business.

Eligha has always known his wife was a sharp woman, but she has always allowed him to lead as the man of the house. Ms. Gwen has shifted the way he sees and deals with all women, including his wife, because Ms. Gwen has taught Eligha a new way to value and interact with women in general. Women have favor and business intellect equal to that of men, and all of us in our society can learn the same lessons. A person's skin color is not the determining factor in a person's character, and neither is their gender.

Chapter 7

Mindset & Revelation

"I want people to believe in themselves, knowing they can do it."

~ E.P.

Eligha's mindset is that your past is in the past – your future is what's ahead. You cannot spend a whole lot of precious time and energy worrying or focusing on the things that occurred in your past. Create your future in your mind, see it clearly, and make it your goal. See yourself in a better job, see yourself in a better position, if you see yourself in a better house, owning your own house even, then set a clear vision of the home in your mind.

Then you must ask God to keep you healthy and ask Him to keep you strong and keep you focused on the road ahead that leads you to your goal. Be mindful of the people who you spend time with and the people you hang out around. Are these people that are on the same path as you? Are these people who will be there to help you achieve your goals or are they leading you off course?

Ask that God surround you with the proper influences and role models, seek out people that help keep your mind focused and on track, and ask that your eyes can see the road and the course ahead that you must travel. Don't stop and never quit. Don't let up or stop until you reach your goal that you set. But when you reach your goal be certain to look back and observe all that God has done for you. Once you make it don't forget where you come from, don't get the 'big head' and say, I did all this by myself. NO. It was not you alone. It was not your genius or your brilliant mind that made it possible, it was and is God and his grace and favor on your journey.

What was Eligha's mindset when he was in the valley, what made him push his way out of the darkness? Prior to his downfall Eligha had never been in the dark valley and he immediately recognized that he did not like it and it was uncomfortable for him. He started to ask himself, how did I get here? How do I get out of here out of this dark place? He thought to himself that he deserved better than the circumstances that he found himself in once he descended into the valley of his downfall. Then he worked hard every day to make a change in his life, "bust a move," like the comedian Robin Harris used to say.

Due to the ordeal back in his hometown right before his dad's diagnosis Eligha was functionally unemployed and completely broke, but he never lost focus of his need to care for his family. At no point did he ever sit around complaining about the things that had happened to him, instead he maintained the same schedule he had since he was a teenager, rising before the sunrise, typically around 4am, beginning his day with a workout in the garage.

Following the announcement by the doctors that his dad only had twenty days to live, Eligha had witnessed his father's miraculous bounce back. This experience launched Eligha on a quest to learn more about how, who, and what had saved his father when he himself was completely helpless to do anything to help his dad. In his mind he thought, "if God allows me to wake up every morning, I am going to get up and keep it pushing." Eligha was determined and driven because he had his own family to take care of and provide for. He had a huge boulder squarely in his path and he purposely kept chipping away at that boulder finding ways to move forward and provide for his family.

Solely because of bearing witness to how God had helped his father recover from stage four cancer when the doctors thought there was no chance, Eligha truly wanted to learn more about the God who had saved his father and he put in the time and energy to do just that. Having never been big on reading, instead of reading the Bible, Eligha played it from CD's as he worked out.

At 4AM one morning, Eligha was in the home gym he had set up in the garage working out and listening to the Bible on CD seeking to learn more about God and his people. Working out has always been a special outlet for Eligha, it is his personal time to work on himself and now it was evolving into a time to also explore his relationship with

God. He walked over to the CD player and pressed play just as he had done for the past few mornings.

With the bible now bellowing from the speakers Eligha walked back to his bench press and started to load up the weights for his first set of lifts. He placed three 45-pound plates, or Cadillacs as they call them, (because they are the biggest plates), on each side of his barbell and settled himself under the weight laying on his back looking up at the 315 pounds poised above his head. One hand reached up and grabbed the bar followed by the other and he hoisted the weight into the air ready to make his first lift. Up and down the massive weight moved with Eligha enjoying the strain he felt across his pecs and up and down his arms.

Folks had often shared with Eligha that God had spoken to them, but up until this point in his life, it had never happened to Eligha. During this 4AM workout session with the Bible playing Eligha openly shares that on this morning, early before the sun had risen while alone in his home gym, he received a revelation[7] from God.

When asked how it happened, how did God speak to you, Eligha shares there was no loud voice, in fact there was no voice at all, no flaming dumbbells or burning bushes in the corner, instead he just knew what God wanted him to know. What was revealed to Eligha was that he was to go back to his hometown and start to build homes again,

---

[7] **Revelation** – where God Himself communicates to you in a way that reflects communication in Heaven. God does not speak in words, ever. And those who think they are hearing his voice are usually hearing the voice of the Holy Spirit possibly mixed with their own inner voice.

building affordable housing in his hometown was his new assignment.

This was a challenging assignment because Eligha was still deeply injured by the events that had occurred in his hometown a few years earlier and he still had no desire to have anything to do with his hometown. But Eligha obeyed. God impressed upon Eligha the areas of his hometown to go to start building again. The areas of town he was directed too were in fact neighborhoods Eligha previously had avoided even as a kid. These were areas of town where he never even drove through for any reason because Eligha had considered them not the best areas at the time.

Yet his directions from God took him into these neighborhoods and directed him to specific locations in those neighborhoods and guess what he found? There were vacant/abandoned lots ready for development and perfect locations for the affordable housing God had instructed Eligha to build. But not only were there available lots, but these lots each had some sort of pre-existing structure on them and because of the pre-existing structure, each lot already had the impact fees paid.

If Eligha were to acquire a completely empty lot and start to build a home from scratch the county would charge two types of impact fees to cover the costs of the impact the new construction would have on the community infrastructure. The first impact fee is for traffic and typically runs about $10k per lot and the second impact fee if for water and typically costs about $8k per lot. Because the lots

Eligha was directed to each had some level of pre-existing structure on them all the associated impact fees were already paid in full and Eligha reaped the benefits of saving about $18k on each lot.

Even more to Eligha's amazement, these lots had signs posted that said, "auction coming soon." Once the lots were identified Eligha had another obstacle which he would have to overcome, how was he going to pay for this new housing project now sitting right in front of him? Eligha pulled out pen and paper and outlined the total costs for buying the lots and placing affordable housing units on the lots per his heavenly instructions. Once he had the entire project planned out on paper, he determined he should present the new development plans to his new mentor, Mr. Frank.

At their next meeting, Eligha shared everything with Mr. Frank in precise detail. He told Mr. Frank how the idea came to him, how he followed the instructions he had received at 4AM in the morning and went out driving around the suggested areas of town. He continued to read Mr. Frank into the fact the once he got into the neighborhoods there were available lots, up for auction, and these lots were not going to have any impact fees because of the pre-existing structures that were in place. Mr. Frank listened intently and Eligha could see him taking it all in and doing calculations in his head.

After Eligha laid out all the details of the project and the total projected costs he sat and waited as Mr. Frank finishing digesting everything he had just been presented and finished running the numbers in his mind. After a brief wait, Mr. Frank shocked Eligha by agreeing to provide all the financing needed to buy the lots and commence the affordable housing construction. This meant that Eligha now had financing.

Because of having to declare bankruptcy when shutting down his home center and general contracting business and all the lawsuits that had been filed by his vendors and subcontractors, he would never have been able to get a conventional bank loan. But Mr. Frank was not a conventional lender, he was a private individual who said yes to Eligha's most unconventional project. Eligha and Mr. Frank now had their second business deal agreed to and ready to get under way.

With his financing now in place, Eligha attended the auctions, and he obtained several lots in these neighborhoods he had been directed to by his 4am revelation. Not only did he place the winning bids for these lots, but the lots were able to be procured for literally pennies on the dollar. A couple of the lots were bought at the auction for less than one thousand dollars apiece. But there was another mental hurdle that Eligha had to overcome, now back in his hometown as a real estate investor, Eligha was quite weary about utilizing his own name and his newly restored license as a builder to come back into town and start building again.

So Eligha made a strategic move. Eligha approached his friend, Sam Butler, to serve as his contractor on his new project. Sam and Eligha had built a relationship when Eligha first started selling insurance. When an insurance client was seeking to purchase a policy to cover their home, the insurance company required the client have what they called a wind-abatement assessment. Eligha would refer his clients to Sam, because one of the services Sam provided was wind-abatement inspections. Sam's wind-abatement business became a regular referral for Eligha, and he and Sam's relationship grew allowing Eligha to learn that Sam was also licensed as a general contractor. Sam also learned a lot about Eligha's past background as a builder.

Once Eligha partnered with Mr. Frank to secure the empty lots for the low-income housing Eligha approached Sam and spoke with Sam about Sam serving as the builder for the homes he had planned for the project. Sam was more than agreeable and knowing of Eligha's past and skill as a developer Sam agreed to serve as the building partner in the new development project. Sam told Eligha he trusted him and knowing that Eligha knew the craft of homebuilding inside and out, whatever Eligha wanted to do with the lots simply place Sam on the paperwork as the contractor and build away. This arrangement allowed Eligha to return to homebuilding, but not under his own name allowing for him to avoid any public notice for the next twelve months or so.

After being led to find these empty lots after his 4AM revelation in the gym, working under Sam's license and with Mr. Frank as his financing partner Eligha completed building brand new affordable homes on all the lots that were purchased at auction. All the homes were successfully sold helping the purchasers become first time homeowners and restarting Eligha's career as a builder once again back in his hometown.

Once that initial project was completed Eligha started searching for his next project and he and Mr. Frank continued to partner with one another developing new real estate projects mostly affordable housing until the day Mr. Frank unexpectedly passed away in 2018. Even with the loss of his friend, mentor, and business partner Mr. Frank's passing did not stop Eligha from continuing to answer the calling he received that fateful morning. He continues to this day to identify great places to build affordable housing in his hometown and to build homes allowing people to become homeowners at a price they otherwise would not be able to afford.

Chapter 8

The Work

For as the body without the spirit is dead, so faith without works is dead also.

James 2:26 (NKJV)

"Well, dear readers, you have come full circle and are back with me, Dina the Angel, and are in Eligha's closet again. What have we learned on this journey?" I hope you now can see how Eligha is one of my favorite humans to observe each day. It is actually a joy to watch anything grow and when a person grows it is pure bliss. Eligha worked hard as a young man. He had a clear vision of what it was he desired out of life. He combined that vision with focused work and he had success.

When he encountered the events of his downfall he was shook. He had to reinvent himself. And he did the work. Every day. He is doing the work today. I would be he will be doing the work tomorrow.

There is a meme floating around the internet that perfectly illustrates the principles of the work.

Tap In: Brick-By-Brick

Many will be familiar with the story of Moses and how he led the nation of Israel of Egypt into the Promised Land. As you may recall Moses was leading the Israelites, a huge multitude of people, through the desert. Some accounts leave the impression that Moses was lost – he was not lost.

Moses was completely tapped into the Divine. He was a highly conscious being, a man of great wisdom and immense understanding. The was a purpose to the multitudes wandering through the wilderness. The time spent wandering allowed for Moses to alter the prevailing attitude of the whole. To erase bad habits, building a new set of practices and understandings as a collective. It was import this take place before they settled in their new land.

One day the people came to their leader. "Moses, we have a problem. We have no water. What are you going to do?" Moses replied addressing the crowd that was gathering around him: "What am I going to do? What are you going to do? Go and pray to your God for rain."

Away the people went. They came back later the following day. "Moses, God has forsaken us!" "What do you mean?" Moses replied. "We did exactly as you asked, we all went to our homes and gathered our families and we all prayed earnestly and faithfully for rain. We prayed and no rain has come. God has forsaken us."

Moses replied: "Tell me, where are the ditches?"

The crowd stood still. There was puzzled silence for some time. It seem they were all confused by Moses' question. Eventually one of them spoke up, "What ditches, why are you asking us where are the ditches, Moses?"

Moses repeated himself, this time in a rhetorical tone, "Where are the ditches? If you believed it was going to rain, you'd have dug the ditches!" The morale of the story should need no further elaboration.

In chapter five of Wallace D. Wattles book, "The Science of Getting Rich" he describes The Intellegent Substance which is all, and in All, and which lives in All and lives in you, is a consciously Living Substance." It is the evident intelligence behind this experience we call life itself. Moses was educating his followers about beliefs and expectation. Put another way, do not expect your God, or anyone else for that matter, to do for you what your God can only do with and through you.

Whatever success looks like to you, here's what you need to ask yourself:

- Are you thinking and acting in harmony with the outcome you desire?
- Where are you digging your ditches?
- Where are you making decisions that prove you believe you're worthy of the level of success you desire?
- What is it you're really expecting and is it really the same as what you tell yourself you are aiming for?

Part of why Moses was teaching was mindset coupled with actions. Changing the way we think is work. Mental work is some of the most exhausting work. Yet, the mental aspect is only part of the secret formula. You have to feel worthy and believe in your vision deep in your soul. This belief vibrates and connects with the pervasive Intelligent Substance. The final ingredient is good old fashion hard work. Lifting something. Writing something. Painting something. Whatever it is, you have to do something. And whatever that something is, it should completely align with you mental work and the vision you've created.

- Are you doing all these things?
- Do you think your internal thoughts, vision, and physical efforts all align?

Here is how you dig your ditches; you put your time, money and energy where your potential is. Each day you seek to improve yourself, Each day you work executing the next step in your plan, the next task on your list. You make yourself bigger and better – in other words, you raise your consciousness – to become a person who is capable of bigger and better results.

Believe. Feel it. Plan your work. Work hard every day.

Remember, **"the riches are in the ditches!"**

Chapter 9

Don't Give Up – Never Quit

"I was motivated to achieve more and believe in myself because I see myself as deserving more and worthy of more."

~ E.P.

Eligha speaks often and we have pulled these E.P. gems together to help keep you energized along the way.

There is a gift and everyone alive on this planet. You must figure out what your gift is. Recognize the favor that allows you to have your gifts come from God. God wants you to exercise your favor and your gifts to help it grow and flourish no matter what your gift is.

To becoming great there is a process. There is a process to everything.

There must be sacrificed because it is not going to be easy

Lock Yourself Down

Sometimes you have to put yourself in jail - you have to incarcerate yourself. All the fun things that you like to do sometimes you have to decide I'm not going out or I'm not going to do blank until I accomplish my goal. If you don't make the necessary sacrifices to accomplish your goal whose fault is it? Use your time wisely.

Tips on How to be successful

1. Develop a close relationship with God. Get to know him.

2. Believe in yourself - tell yourself affirming statements that reinforce your goal." I Want To Be My Own Boss." Print your affirmations out on a piece of paper and post it somewhere you'll see it every day. Place it near your sink or by your desk. So you can see your goal every day. If you have a mentor or an example you're seeking to be like place a picture of that person up somewhere where you can see it. Keep yourself focused on your goals and the task at hand.

When making his comeback from his Fall From Grace Elijah focused on customer service. Great customer service was a Cornerstone of building Elijah's Insurance business into the number to agent in the whole country. At one point Elijah had an insurance office inside of JoJo Wings, He would meet us customers there and when inspired he would pay for their meal or help them out with their bills always staying engage with the customer. Be kind. Be nice. Be understanding. Use a sense of humor. Always understand that the customer is the reason that you are in business stay focused on showing your appreciation that's how Eligha built his insurance business.

Don't be surprised when other people do not celebrate your gift, keep pushing, and keep exercising your gift knowing the rewards will come. Keep pushing - look good, smell good, believe in yourself, and keep on pushing.

Life is a blessing. Sometimes you have to encourage yourself even a bad day is one more day to fulfill your purpose and be a blessing to others.

How do you keep it- how do you stay successful?

1. Understand where your blessings and your favor come from. They come from God.

2. You must be a blessing to others. The more you are blessed the more important this principle becomes. You can only continue to be blessed if you have an open hand. As you receive your blessings you must release them. Inspiring others, helping others, and blessing others are keys to success. It does not always have to be money - you can bless others by sharing your testimony with them orb I'm entering another person.

www.ingramcontent.com/pod-product-compliance
Lightning Source LLC
Chambersburg PA
CBHW052231230426
43666CB00035B/2654